glimpses *of* tenderness

Soothing the Soul
Through Reminiscence

LORI MYERS

This book is dedicated to my husband, my children, and my mom. Their never-ending support and encouragement of my writing pursuits provide me the motivation and determination to realize my life-long dream of becoming an author. Each of you inspires me to be a better person!

This book is also dedicated to God who instilled in my heart the yearning to soothe the hearts of others by allowing me to share my own stories of loss and grief. Through His grace, I have discovered vulnerability, comfort, and healing.

PREFACE

I am not going to ask how you are doing or how are you coping with your loss. Instead, I will ask you to share a story about your loved one.

Several years ago, my family and I suffered several consecutive losses, all painfully tragic. The flurry started in 2006 with the death of my mother-in-law, Gail, also known as Nanny, to emphysema; in 2008, my ex-husband—the father of my daughters—was shot and killed by a police officer. In late 2009, just seven months after being diagnosed with ALS (also known as Lou Gehrig's disease), we lost my dad—my hero—and then four years later, my thirty-two-year-old daughter-in-law passed away from an amniotic fluid embolism, a rare and often fatal condition experienced in childbirth.

A dear friend recently asked me how I stayed strong and coped, let alone functioned, after so many losses, one after another. My first response to her was "with prayer." Only through God do I find the strength to navigate the flood of emotions experienced during times of loss. Mind you, this is not just my prayers, but also the prayers of so many loving, caring family members and friends. I then shared with her how I find great comfort while reminiscing about lost loved ones.

Recounting details leading up to or directly following the loss of a dear one reminds me of ways that person touched my life. While reminiscing, it is amazing how one can find glimpses of tenderness, happiness, and joy in the hardest of times.

Intentionally wandering through distant memories soothes the sting of loss.

When you have stories to share of those who have gone on ahead, they will always be in your heart. Let me share a few of mine!

INTRODUCTION

At fourteen years old, I found the concept of grief perplexing. I could not understand how this human condition, which inevitably happens to every one of us, could bring so much sorrow. To me, these reactions are not practical.

By the time I was an official teenager, I had experienced three significant deaths. At seven, I was awakened in the middle of the night by a shrill scream. This is when I first realized a phone call in the middle of the night brings no good news. My mother, only twenty-four at the time, had lost her father. Her grief was deep and touched every one of us. When I found out I could not attend the funeral, I felt left out. I wanted to see my grandpa. "You're too young to understand" was the justification.

At nine, my fraternal grandmother passed. I was close to her, closer than any of my four younger siblings. Her gracious Southern upbringing was ever-present in her gentle and kind demeanor. She was the rock and foundation of her family. My parents let me go to her funeral. By age nine, I guess one is old enough to experience this ritual. Except, no one prepared me for what the experience would entail. I didn't know I would see her body—lifeless, colorless, motionless. I did not understand why the essence of her was absent from her physical being.

Then at thirteen, my fraternal grandfather died. My dad was sad but didn't project the profound sadness he had when his mother died. My grandfather was a man I never knew. He had been in a VA hospital since before I had been born. I had heard the stories of how his cruel drunkenness had left my grandmother to raise ten children while working several odd jobs. This loss was void of any real emotion. My sadness was for my dad because now, he had no living parents.

The next loss came after I questioned grief. When I was sixteen, my last grandparent died of Huntington's disease. Due to her declining mental condition, which prevented her from caring for herself, she resided in a state hospital for the last several years of her life. Three years before her passing, my family made the 150-mile drive to visit her. She was not the woman I remembered. My mom told us that her sickness had affected her memory and reactions, and she experienced occasional outbursts. I could not understand how the body could become so lifeless while it was still alive. When she passed, my mother shed no tears. I believed my mom was a monster for not crying. *You are supposed to cry; after all, she was your mother!* Many years later, I learned why my mother didn't cry. She explained, "You don't shed tears for a woman you'd never wish back to this earth . . . not the way she had come to be." It was then I realized how deeply my mother had loved her mom.

For most children, these events may pass in some matter-of-fact way. For me, they formed a foundational mindset of inquiry. Each death was a mystery and something for me to ponder. Much later in my life, I would learn that a loss is a loss, regardless of the event—death, divorce, a broken relationship, being fired from a job . . . the list goes on.

My significant losses came much later in my life. Not only because of the nature of my relationships but because of the tragedy that surrounded each loss. Older people weren't dying because their bodies gave out. In some cases, they were young people who died too soon.

I recently shared my teenage views of death with

my son: my lack of understanding about why we're not geared, or at least conditioned, to handle our inevitable endings. He offered a notion I had never considered. When the Lord created man and woman, we were promised immortality. The promise of eternity is written on our souls. We forfeited the promise for knowledge and independence when we bought into the serpent's lie. It is that original promise that we mourn. That is the void we all seek to fill.

Of all my pondering, this was the most plausible theory I had ever heard. It made sense to me. This explains why we experience so much sorrow when it comes to death. We mourn for a loss we can never regain in this life.

Where does that leave us? I believe it comes back to our faith. Our faith that says one day we will be reunited with those lost loved ones in a place that has no grief, sorrow, or tears.

With this notion, a loss is a temporary separation. It is a curtain that separates us from the other side. We feel the weight of that separation because of time, an instrument used to measure everything. I am sure the concept of time does not exist in heaven.

I choose to write about several of my losses in a way that captures some essence about each person.

Through my storytelling, I share something special about them to honor them and so others can relate to the gravity of the grief condition, but also gain some peace amongst all that emotion.

SOUNDS OF HOME

*D*usk nears on a late October day in 2009. The brilliant colors of a North Carolina fall, filled with rustling leaves and gentle warmth, bring little comfort now. I rush from my office in Charlotte after a long, stressful day to my daily visit with Dad and Mom in the little town of Mount Holly.

My brother and I moved to this area from central New York in the mid-90s. A few years later, after Mom retired, my parents joined us here. For me, it was a new beginning—a new job with less travel and a new place where my kids could have a better life. For Dad and Mom, it brought the opportunity to be near their youngest grandchildren, my two girls, and my brother's four kids. Dad and Mom's entire married life of fifty years revolved around their family—Sunday dinners, holidays, vacations, and even the decision about where to live.

My dad grew up in northern New York State. He was the eighth child of ten, and by all standards, considered extremely poor. Though they didn't have much growing up and faced hardships brought on by an alcoholic father, it was the kind, gentle, loving spirit of his mother that made him the unselfish, devoted husband and father he became.

I often referred to my dad as that unassuming, passive fellow you wouldn't pick out in a crowd. What the masses didn't know was just how special he was. To this day, each of his five children and many grandchildren can recite countless memories filled with laughter, shenanigans, and connectedness.

These days, I desperately cling to the fleeting moments when my parents are together; they have always been together. At seventy-two, I'm glad my dad has enjoyed more than ten years of retirement from his job at General Motors, where he was a loyal and dedicated employee for nearly thirty years. Not a surprise for a man who always demonstrated love and commitment to his family, always putting the needs of others above himself.

Until now, I didn't really understand the concept of "living in the moment." These days, I find myself grasping at that notion. Time has taken on a new meaning!

No one answers the door when I knock. In the many years that Mom and Dad have lived in this quaint, little brick house, the front door has always been open, from the time when their five noisy kids were running in and out and through more recent days. Dad loves the way the brilliant North Carolina sunshine baths the front room in the late afternoon. But now, the door is always closed.

As I open the door, I'm not greeted by warm welcomes. The room is dark. The TV plays much louder than I ever remember, even when they had a house full of kids and half the neighborhood inside. Dad's hearing is not so good these days, though it is amazing how he occasionally detects whispered conversations from the next room. Is the TV loud to give Dad some sense of normal or is it to mask the reality of what his life has become? How astute the senses are when your world shrinks to the confines of a tiny, one thousand square-foot house.

What I do not hear is Dad calling for me from his usual spot in the dining room. In recent days, I'd find him there, ciphering the household budget or diligently working a jumble from the morning paper. There he'd sit with a cup of cold coffee that he'd been drinking for hours, sporting his '80s-style reading glasses, and wearing what the family calls his current uniform—worn blue jeans and a crisp, white Fruit-of-the-Loom t-shirt. Dad always liked a uniform, be it the Air Force blues he wore as an Air Policeman in the 1950s or his factory outfit of slacks and a button-down shirt.

The quiet, empty dining room allows me a moment to reflect on happier times—times from my childhood—when Dad was well. Warm summer and fall days were spent enjoying outdoor childhood games: dodge ball, kickball, and our favorite, hide-and-seek. My thoughts wander back to the summer after I turned thirteen.

Twilight is approaching. Twelve neighborhood kids hurry through dinner. Everyone is anxious to start the nightly game of hide-and-seek. My house is the perfect place to play. It sits in the middle of a city park, surrounded by large trees and dense bushes. The absence of streetlights adds to the neighborhood's darkness. Oh, how we love the thrill of playing a game where you hide in the dark!

The best hiding spots are well known. Each child hoping to find that one place where he can fake out the "seeker." Darkness comes. We gather in the field restlessly waiting to start the game.

Throughout the game, I am laser-focused on avoiding that tap on the shoulder, accompanied by a loud shout of "You're it!"

[Back then, Dad was part of our game.] *He peeks out of the living room window. Always the prankster, he enjoys times when he can surprise us. More times than not, his goal is to scare us.* [Trust me, he was good at that.] *He carefully creeps out of the house through the cellar door. He slides behind an eight-foot rock wall that towers on the opposite side of the field where we play. No one hides behind that old wall because it is in plain sight.*

As another game starts, frenzied kids, trying to avoid being caught, run in every direction. Dad uses this chaotic moment to move into position. He plans to jump out at just the right moment to scare as many kids as possible. And boy, does he!

Imagine a stampede of kids taking off at break speed, all trying to get to the safety of the nearest house— my house. Though I am first through the door, I quickly find myself underfoot, literally. Every kid in the neighborhood is running over the top of me, as I remain sprawled out on the hallway floor. Everyone is screaming for Dad to come help: "Dad!" "Jack!"

"Mr. Trainham!" all being shouted in unison, including Mom, who heard all the commotion from her spot in the kitchen. [Oh, how we wailed in surprise and disbelief when we found out that DAD was the bogyman himself! He was always there to save us from whatever stirred in the dark.]

The absence of Dad sitting in the dining room jolts me back to today's reality. Nearly forty years later, he cannot play hide-and-seek or any other summer game. He is not sitting in his usual spot. Now, he spends most of his time in a hospital bed, barely making a sound. He no longer sips cold coffee or jumps out from the perfect hiding place, shouting, "BOO!"

Instead, the undertone of the house is the slow, steady hiss of Dad's oxygen machine, intermingled with the repetitive injection from the "Joey," his feeding machine. What I wouldn't give to hear Dad tell any of a dozen old Air Force stories from when he was stationed in Morocco (for the hundredth time) or his retelling of all the playful pranks he pulled on us over the years. Aside from the life-sustaining machines, the house is eerily quiet now.

Mom calls from the kitchen, "Lori, is that you?" She is now the one who ciphers—keeping track of each hour of the day and the correct dose of medication for Dad's next round. Our usual, easy conversation barely begins. Mom worries she will miss Dad's whispered call. ALS usually manifests in the limbs, and patients lose their ability to walk. Five to ten percent of those with ALS lose their ability to swallow and speak. Some may have frontal lobe issues, which affect their ability to think, to reason. This is how it showed up for Dad. His speech this last year has been defined by just a few words and always as whispers. How painful it must be to lose your voice!

As Mom rushes from the kitchen to Dad's bedside, I become keenly aware of the steady rhythm of a small clock on the mantle. For them, time is no longer marked by the hour they go to dinner or by the TV guide's schedule of their favorite shows but by doctors' appointments, clinic visits, and the next time hospice will come.

Time is no longer measured by the sweeping motion of the second hand but rather by the depth of emotion each quiet moment evokes.

The usual bustle of Mom and Dad's home had

been playfully chaotic, no matter where or how they lived. They've always shared their home with their kids, grandchildren, and a little barking Yorkie. Gone are the youthful summer days and the echoes of the lively home that made me who I am. Gone are the spirited debates over the latest social controversy, the colorful opinions on national politics, or the hardy laughter shared by the retelling of Dad's silly pranks.

The once-thriving heartbeat of their home is overshadowed by the steady hum of a disease for which there is no triumph. The busy, bustling sounds of home are replaced with unsettling sounds of illness and long stints of silence.

Rather than succumb to the sadness of this time, I have come to appreciate the silent moments. In those quiet times, I daydream about carefree days filled with love and laughter. Precious memories of a wonderful childhood bring tremendous comfort now. Remembering Dad in his youth, always a kid at heart, calms the overwhelming anxiousness I feel as his passing approaches. Memories of a noisy, animated childhood home filled with playful memories sustain me as I once again face what hides in the dark!

*JACK WAYNE TRAINHAM was born in Carthage, New York in 1937. This was my Dad, my hero! He died a few days before Christmas in 2009 from complications brought on by ALS—just seven months after the diagnosis. He did not lose the use of his legs as most do from this disease; he did lose his voice several months before he died. Strong thoughts, feelings, and emotions could not be spoken, simply written down on scraps of paper. One day, I will share, in story form, the love, devotion, and wonder left behind on those little scraps of paper.

2

NANNY'S GARDEN

A warm breeze caresses my aching spirit as I stretch out on a comfy, worn-out old chaise in Nanny's garden. It has been another stressful week. Too many meetings, too many deadlines, and way too many people with urgent demands. My nearly thirty years in the corporate rat race with never-ending stress is taking its toll. I have recently realized how important it is to take a break, disconnect from the chaos, be present, and breathe. Spending time here in Nanny's garden relaxes me. Lounging here reminds me of how this garden came to be such a loving, warm, comforting place. Gosh, I need a nap!

As I begin drifting off to sleep, I hear the flutter of hummingbird wings. I close my eyes and barely move a muscle. I slow my breathing. In my mind's eye, I trace the rapid movement of those little wings. They move so fast but don't appear to move at all. The little bird zigzags around the garden, hovering in flight, moving quickly from one flower to the next. This rushed rhythm is repeated until he finally decides it's time to disappear. Once he has his fill of sweet floral nectar, off he goes to destinations unknown.

Nanny loved to watch the hummingbirds. As a Southern woman, she knew exactly what flowers to have in the garden to keep them coming back year after year: bee balm, petunias, salvia, and zinnia.

Their orchestrated dance brought Nanny much joy, especially in her last days during the summer of 2006.

Even with labored breath brought on by emphysema, Nanny found the strength to prop herself up in the hospital bed that dominated the sitting room once used for lively family gatherings. From that position, she could watch those tiny little birds through the large bay window overlooking her spectacular garden.

I only got to know Nanny six years before she

passed. She was naturally beautiful—silky skin, blushed cheeks, and blue eyes the color of the Carolina sky. Her most striking feature was her ever-present dimples brought about by her warm and welcoming smile. Nanny was graceful, poised, and sharp as a tack. She was not afraid to speak her mind and always allowed me to speak mine. I learned from her what it was like to be a strong, determined woman, one who accomplished whatever she set her mind to. I miss her!

That west-facing window was such a gift! Each morning, Poppy pulled open the heavy brocade drapes before the sun rose. Even in the twilight, the garden shone brightly. Thankfully, Nanny could peer out that window throughout the day since the hot North Carolina sun did not arrive until late afternoon. Over fifty years ago, Poppy promised Nanny to be there for better or worse, in sickness and in health. His adoration for Nanny was evident in every action he took to make her as comfortable as possible. Poppy never left her side!

Gazing at the garden and all its activity brought Nanny much joy. Whenever possible, she would share stories of how the garden came to be—her travels to find just the right selection of roses, how she mapped out the placement of flowers so their colors rightly complemented one another, and the decisions she faced when adding various trees. After all, it was important for the trees to give the right amount of shade over the gazebo where the family would often gather. Nanny placed a stainless-steel gazing ball in the center of the garden where the cardinals, blue jays, and hummingbirds could admire themselves. The garden was made even more enchanting by the copper wind chimes that softly echoed in the breeze.

As a child growing up in rural North Carolina, Nanny spent many a day in her grandmother's garden. This was a place where she could be anyone she wanted to be. She and her sister Jean would have playful tea parties where they pretended to be grand princesses from the olden days. They would lie in the lush grass and listen to chickadees and doves chirping while trying to guess the names of the flowers responsible for the wonderful aroma. Whenever Nanny came upon honeysuckle, you could see in her eyes that she was taken back to that place she so loved.

Nanny's garden was spectacular, more beautiful than her childhood dreams ever imagined it could be. It was like a Thomas Kincaid painting, where light illuminated from every angle. The delicate flowers displayed the vibrant colors of the South: red, yellow, blue, lilac, and orange. They were a breath-taking invitation for hummingbirds, butter-flies, cardinals, and the occasional weary soul.

As the afternoon sunbathes my face, another warm breeze slips through the fingers of the garden's wind chimes. The sound is like tiny angels playing a lullaby. If you listen closely, you can tell which direction the wind is blowing by the different tones of the chimes. Nanny never complained or tired of these chimes, even when they awakened her from what had become deep slumbers.

On the day Nanny passed, Poppy was at her side. The room was dim, the air was heavy but still, and the garden was in full bloom. We were not ready to say goodbye, but Nanny was where she wanted to be —at home with Poppy overlooking the magnificent garden she had created, cultivated, and cared for with love and tenderness.

Though Nanny no longer gazes upon this earthly garden, I am comforted by this place that continues to give refuge through its beauty. Nanny taught me that strength can be quiet and graceful. She taught me how to show love through God's natural gifts. This place holds the perfect combination of energy and tranquility. As slumber covers me, the sounds of the hummingbird's wings and the wind chime's angelic song bring me much needed peace.

*GAIL CATO MYERS was born in North Carolina. She died on Flag Day in 2006 from emphysema. She was housebound the last year of her life, much of that time confined to her bed. Though her liveliness was no longer evident in movement; it was there in her conversations and in her smile. From the moment we met, Nanny and Poppy treated me and my daughters like we were part of their family. She showed me the same Southern graceful comfort and love my Gramma did; a love I represented in this garden.

3

A SOFT LAP

*I*t was a summer afternoon like most when Marie visited her grandparents in the North Country. All the neighborhood kids were running around playing tag, hopscotch, jumping rope, riding bikes, or gliding down the sidewalk in roller skates that slipped over your shoes and had a key to tighten the fit.

Marie was so caught up in a game of tag, she barely heard her mom say, "If we are not back by the time the streetlights go on, go to Mrs. Busler's house." What seven-year-old pays any attention to a grown-up when engrossed in a game of tag? She vaguely recalled the old Buick station wagon pulling away.

Marie and her friends played game after game with barely a notion of time. One by one, kids ran home. Some were called by a loud shout from their dad; some knew it was time to go because the streetlights came on. Before she knew it, Marie was the only one left in the alleyway. No one shouted her name. Marie realized she had never been outside in the dark alone!

Marie wandered back to Gramma B's porch. She sat in the twilight for what seemed like hours. She kept replaying pieces of her mother's words. "Did Mom say to go in the house? Surely, she did not want me to sit in the dark until they got home."

Maybe Mom and Dad lost track of time. "I will just sit here for a bit. I am sure they will be here soon!" Marie did not wear a watch—what seven-year-old kid does? She had no concept of time. All she knew was that it was dark, eerily quiet, and there was not a soul around.

Marie's thoughts moved to action. "I can't just sit here and do nothing." She tried to open the front and back doors of the house. No luck. All the doors were locked. She thought of going to a neighbor's house but was not sure if her mom and dad would approve of that since she barely knew those families. She sat for a bit more.

Then a brilliant idea came to Marie. Her other Gramma, Gramma T, lived just a few blocks away. She would just walk over to her house. She had walked it many times with her dad—ever since she was a toddler—and knew the route well.

Marie traced the path in her head – she'd walk quickly past the two old dogs down the street whose bark was meant to keep out trespassers, turn left at the end of the street, go three blocks, cross over the train tracks, then turn left. Gramma T's house was the white two-story townhouse on the right.

Marie took a deep breath and opened her eyes. She jumped off the stoop with determination, briskly pumping her little legs while counting every step. Counting while walking always took her mind off the distance. With each step, she grew more confident and courageous and, somehow, more determined to get where she was going.

By now, all the streetlights were lit; their pale-yellow glow gave enough light to take the fear out of the journey. Thankfully, the lights were scattered all the way up the street in a crisscross pattern. Marie made a game of getting from one bright spot to the next. Her pace picked up and the length in her steps got wider. "I'll get to Gramma's house in no time."

Suddenly, Marie heard a bark in the distance. Faint at first, then stronger as the sound grew closer. Marie's heart pumped faster, matching her quickening steps. She did not know much about dogs. Dad brought home a dog once but trying to keep up with four little kids and a dog was more than Mom and Dad wanted to juggle. What little she knew was that someone usually got bit. As her legs moved faster, the sound faded. She did not give in to panic or fear. She did not give in to the urge to run; she just listened and kept up her determined pace.

Before she knew it, Marie had turned the block and was approaching the train tracks. This area was darker since there were no streetlights on this stretch. Marie recalled all her dad taught her about train tracks - step quickly but carefully so as not to trip.

Suddenly a story Dad told her about these tracks snapped into her thoughts. "Marie, when my brother Kenny was six years old, he and his buddy John were playing on the train tracks. They were told this was dangerous, but they did what boys do, they made an adventure out of jumping from track to track. When reaching down to pick up a bent penny on the track, a blasting cap exploded in Kenny's face. He lost an eye. He tried to make a game of his loss. Every night he put his glass eye in the cup on the nightstand between our beds. I've always remembered the lesson he learned for the rest of us: step swiftly and don't play on the tracks."

No fear of playing on the tracks tonight. Marie did not jump the treads, as she and her little sister

Eve sometimes did despite Dad's warning. She slowed as she neared the tracks, being sure to stay several feet from the first rail. She leaned forward to listen for the deafening whistle and the glaring headlight of the engine. She heard nothing but the sound of a million crickets. Marie stayed there for what felt like an eternity, breathing slowly and listening deeply. Finally, she knew it was time to make a dash across the rails as quickly as she could to get to the other side. One, two, three . . . *GO!*

Marie was flooded with relief as she made it to the other side. She stopped just long enough to catch her breath. Then she noticed her untied sneaker. Rather than spend any time imaging that she could have fallen (as her mother so often said would be her fate for not tying her shoe), she tied it and moved on. She could see the streetlight at the corner of Gramma T's street.

When Marie rounded the corner, she burst into a mad dash and nearly crashed when she hit the front porch stairs. She saw the soft, green-tinged light from the funny lamp that sat on the sofa table in the living room. Marie knew she was safe again.

Marie knocked on the door. No one came. "What if Gramma isn't home?" She wondered what to do next. Taking a deep breath, she knocked again, this time a little harder.

A few seconds later, a soft voice asked who was there. "Gramma, it's me, Marie. Mom and Dad went shopping with my other Gramma. I was left playing at the house, then everyone went home. I was alone in the dark and didn't know what do to."

Gramma slowly opened the door to find her little Marie disheveled and slightly out of breath. Gramma first asked if Marie was OK, then she asked if she was hungry. To that Marie exclaimed, "I haven't eaten in forever! Can I have some tea, too?"

Marie frantically chattered away about the game of tag, mom's faint directions of what to do, and the empty street. She spoke of all the emotion she felt while sitting on the porch alone and of the courage she mustered to walk to Gramma's house. Some parts got bigger and louder, like the barking dog, the scary train tracks, and the millions of crickets.

When Marie's energy about the adventure subsided, it was clear she was worried about her parents. Her rapid-fire questions gave way to more uncertainty and anxiousness. Gramma knew just what to do—what she always did when Marie was sleepy or upset. Gramma sat Marie down in her rocker and went off to the kitchen to get a slice of hot apple pie she'd just pulled from the oven and some hot tea.

Marie often watched Gramma fry chicken, roast

pork for barbeque sandwiches, and use lots of lard in her pie crusts. She especially loved Gramma's apple pies. The smell of cinnamon filled the air and reminded her of all the love Gramma put into everything she cooked. And the hot tea . . . always made with two teaspoons of sugar and some cream, just the way Gramma drank it. She quickly gobbled up the pie and slowly sipped the tea until her teacup was empty.

Gramma pulled Marie onto her lap and rocked her as she had when Marie was a baby. It did not matter that Marie was bigger now and probably all kinds of dirty from playing games and trekking through the night air. Granma knew how to soothe her anxiousness.

With the rocking and Gramma's singing a soft lullaby in the room with the green lamp casting its warm hue, Marie began to settle down.

Rocking babies was something Gramma had been doing for a long time. She had ten children and many more grandchildren. She made every one of those children and "grands" feel special. Gramma T. sent cards on every birthday, made meals steeped in

Southern tradition for every occasion, and prayed that all of us would have good lives and much love. She passed on those values and qualities to her children, including Marie's dad who was eighth in line.

Gramma was born at the turn of the century. She was the oldest of three children and raised in a modestly affluent family that followed Methodist and Southern traditions. Gramma arrived in upstate New York as a young bride of a U.S. Army soldier who was also from Virginia. They had met and married when she was just sixteen. Shortly after the birth of their first child, Grampa was transferred to Fort Drum in Watertown, New York. This was quite a culture shock for Gramma, who had never left the state of Virginia.

Though she had been in New York for nearly fifty years, Gramma still had that melodic southern Virginia accent. She was the epitome of Southern grace—God-fearing, gentle-hearted, and soft-spoken. Gramma never cursed or talked gossip. She was proud of her roots and shared many stories of her childhood in the small town of Blackstone.

Gramma's adult life was far from easy. Sometimes, she had to take on as many as three jobs to care for her family. Jobs like bookkeeper and housekeeper, and she even worked as a wet nurse. Her determination and dedication to caring for her family, no matter the circumstances, was most respected by her family. All who knew Gramma, loved Gramma!

There was a Grampa, but his work was never steady because of injuries he had suffered in a war many years ago. Marie never met her Grampa. He had been in a Veteran's hospital since before her birth. His absence never seemed odd. It was just the way it was.

The slow, steady rocking in the soft light as Gramma hummed a Southern lullaby was all Marie needed to completely settle down. Gone was the anxiousness and hunger. Just as she started to drift off to sleep, she heard a knock at the door. Marie quickly jumped off Gramma's lap quickly when she saw the door opening and heard her dad's voice say, "Mom, it's Jack and Marty."

Marie felt relieved. All was right now. Mom and Dad were there. Dad said, "Marie, we're so glad we found you. We were all so worried. Mrs. Butler said you didn't come home with the kids after you were all done playing. How in the world did you get here?"

A quick thought came to Marie. "Mrs. Butler's house? Boy, I missed that part!" She turned to her mom and said, "I'm OK, Mom. I sat for a bit then walked myself here. It was dark and kind of scary, but Gramma made me apple pie and tea. She sang to me in her rocker, like she did when I was a little girl. I'm OK . . . really!"

Marie's mom and dad hugged her like they had not seen her in years. She was happy to be safe again and proud of the journey she made from one Gramma's house to the other. It never occurred to her to be afraid, only determined.

Marie's belief in herself to face a scary situation came from her father's teachings, which had come down from her beloved Gramma. Through simple, loving gestures of food, song, and the quiet motion of a rocking chair, Gramma's love soothed Marie's anxious heart. The memories of fifty years ago bring the same sense of confidence, calmness, and courage.

*BERTHA WATSON TRAINHAM (GRAMMA T) was born in 1904 in Blackstone, Virginia. Her affluent childhood in a loving Southern home gave her grace and humility. Married at sixteen to a man thirteen years her senior, she had ten children over the course of twenty years. Most of her adult life was filled with strife brought on from life with an alcoholic. She always remained loving, nurturing, and caring. Gramma passed a couple of months before my tenth birthday. This loss was pivotal in my life and informed much of my thinking about death and loss. Her life has always reminded me that we can be kind, caring, and selfless despite life's adversities and trials.

4

HELL ON WHEELS

The day starts like most any other day. Thomas wakes up early to the aroma of freshly baked danishes. As he shuffles into the warm kitchen, he is greeted with a hearty *"Guten Morgen"* by his Oma. Only three years old, Thomas knows little more of the world than the busy, bustling farmhouse, German tales and lullabies, and the love of his maternal Oma.

Thomas's mother, Ursula, holds a special place in his heart, as well. He spends little time with her, but what time they have is filled with love. Ursula's dream of being a world-class Olympic swimmer was dashed when she became pregnant at seventeen by a young U.S. serviceman stationed in Germany. She was barely into her pregnancy when that young man was redeployed to Vietnam and never heard from again. It was always assumed he had no knowledge of Ursula's pregnancy when he left. After Thomas was born, Ursula had no choice but to leave him in her mother's care while she worked long days in a nearby city.

Thomas did not leave Oma's side. The days on the farm were filled with many chores—tending to the chickens and goats, taking care of the garden, cooking, baking meals to feed Thomas's large family, and all the other things people do to keep a farm running. No matter the task at hand, Oma always had a tale to tell or a song to sing. Her lightheartedness filled the void of Thomas's days spent without his mom.

Then one day, Ursula burst into the kitchen beaming with joy. She picked Thomas up and swirled around and around. She kissed him on the cheek and said, "Thomas, today you will go on a great adventure. You and I will be flying to America! You will see so many wonderful sights and meet your American family." Though Oma had never been to America, she shared with Thomas a story or two about the wonders he would see.

Ursula had met and married Marty, another U.S. serviceman who was stationed at the U.S. Army Garrison in Heidelberg. His tour in Germany was over, and they were all heading stateside. Thomas barely knew his new stepfather and certainly nothing about America. All Thomas knew was that today he was dressed in his finest German lederhosen—suede leather shorts—and had to be extra careful not to get his breakfast all over them.

Thomas ran to Oma and asked if she was coming to America with them. She stroked his blond curls and looked deep into his soft brown eyes and said, "No, my love. I need to stay on the farm to care for Opa and your uncles." She patted his little chest and told him that she would always be right there, in his heart, just as he would always be in her heart. Then, she swept him up in her arms and gave him a hug to last a lifetime.

When the farmhouse door closed behind Thomas and Ursula, that would be the end of the warmth, safety, and love that had filled Thomas's life those three short years. No longer would his days contain laughter and song. The trip to America with the man he barely knew and a mom that had popped in and out of his life on weekends would prove to be a significant turning point for young Thomas.

Not only was America so different from anything Thomas had known, he did not understand anything people said to him. He could not speak English and no one other than his mother spoke German. Thomas's vocabulary was limited to that of a three-year-old. Ursula had to translate every conversation, and if she was not around, he had few ways to communicate. For the first time in Thomas's short life, he felt alone and disconnected.

Despite the loneliness, at first, America was a fun place. Marty took Thomas to Philadelphia Phillies baseball games on Saturday afternoons. These outings were such a treat—with hot dogs and popcorn—and the stands offered excitement unlike anything Thomas had ever known. After all, organ music and the noise of a happy crowd are universally understood sounds, regardless of language.

Thomas's new American family was large, like his German family. Marty had seven sisters and brothers. Thomas's new Grandmom was hard, just like the streets of South Philadelphia where she was from. She raised her kids alone after losing her husband shortly after the birth of her youngest daughter. Grandmom was direct and never pulled any punches, but her love for her family was strong and deep. She immediately accepted Thomas as one of her own.

The next ten years were filled with turmoil. A few more siblings came along, as did the big move from South Philly to the New Jersey suburbs, just over the Walt Whitman bridge. These were not happy years for Thomas. The more kids there were, the less time his mother had for him. And even though Marty had taken him to ballgames, Thomas's relationship with Marty had always been contentious and filled with awful situations too difficult to share. His feelings of being alone and disconnected deepened further since his first days in America.

Thomas was too young to remember that Marty was not his biological dad. He always knew he was treated differently than the other kids, but it never crossed his mind to ask why. The love Thomas experienced in his first three years from his Oma seemed to have vanished but later, he realized it had remained deep within his core.

At thirteen, Thomas was finally going back home to Germany to visit Oma and his German family. He could barely sit still on the long plane ride. He spent much of that time reciting what German he could remember, which was mostly the lyrics to lullabies his Oma and mom had sung to him at bedtime.

The farmhouse was not like he remembered. Opa had passed a few years before. His uncles had moved to the city, all except Dieter. The farm seemed smaller. The animals were gone, and the garden had morphed into a brown patch of weeds. The once vibrant energy of the working farm that had filled his life and now his memories was muted. Thankfully, when the farmhouse door flew open, Oma's smile was as warm as the aroma of freshly baked bread that still hung in the air.

After Opa passed, Dieter returned home to help Oma take care of the farm. He was blonde-haired, tall, and strong. His stride screamed of confidence, and his heavily accented English was melodic. Thomas was most enamored with his quiet demeanor. Though Thomas barely understood German and could make out little of what Dieter said, those sounds instantly reminded him of the loving and comforting days from his early childhood. The love he felt on that little German farm somewhat dulled the sting of his life in America.

That summer, Thomas was introduced to a 1948 panhead Harley Davidson. All his uncles rode motorcycles. Dieter had several other motorcycles, but this one was special. He shined and polished it after every ride and treated it like a museum piece.

Thomas learned to ride a motorcycle—not the panhead of course. He learned on a beat-up, old low rider. Dieter didn't mind if that motorcycle was dumped from time to time. Thomas was also introduced to "colors," the jacket patches from the German motorcycle club that Dieter wore proudly on his well-worn brown leather jacket.

From that day on, Thomas was hooked on motorcycles—but not just any motorcycle; it had to be a

Harley Davidson. Though it would be years before he got his first HD, after that summer in Germany he became a biker at heart. Anyone who knows a true biker knows that it is more than a mode of transportation or a shiny toy; it is a lifestyle, an image, one's essence.

For Thomas, his motorcycle was a shield, which he used to protect himself from the hurts of home and the world.

Thomas's motorcycle was the one thing that, no matter the hardship or circumstance, he could hold onto—an object of strength and invincibility. A bike gave him confidence and courage, which mostly showed up in the form of recklessness, all ways of nonconformity, and sadly, addictions of all sorts.

Several years after that transformative summer, Thomas received a package from Dieter. It was the gas tank from Dieter's 1948 panhead, along with his colors from his riding jacket. Thomas was awestruck! These things became his most cherished possessions . . . along with the little German shorts he wore on that long plane ride to America.

At age twenty-five, Thomas bought his first motorcycle (bike). He could ride to his heart's content. No longer did he sit on landscaped slopes overlooking busy highways, daydreaming of the open road. He could now find the places where he fit in. Places where his story was not the worst story there was to tell. Places where people didn't judge him for the clothes he wore, the money he made, or the job he had. Bikers just like him, living their lives their own way, no matter what others thought. And sadly, that also meant living in ways that brought harm to him or others.

Thomas tried to live like a "citizen." Citizen was his word for anyone that conformed to societal norms, someone who never took risks, or an individual who lacked substance. He knew this was the accepted path and the one taken by most. Thomas struggled to stay on that path. Alcohol and drugs numbed the pain of the childhood he experienced since leaving Germany, the loss of trust for so many when he learned at 20 that Marty wasn't his biological dad, and the disconnected feeling that was always present.

As a result of those demons, Thomas often found himself on the wrong side of the law. His actions suggested he lacked a sense of wrongdoing. One may have said he cared little for those affected by his reckless behavior. I am certain this tied back to the biker mentality—the strength and invincibility he used to deflect his inner pain.

For the next twenty years, Thomas tried to live a life of conformity. He lived with his wife and kids in a house in the suburbs and owned a family pet or two. This kind of life kindled the memories of his childhood that had been so deeply buried inside him. No matter what demons he fought—drugs, alcohol, fighting—his love for his children ran deeper than any other emotion he felt.

Thomas never felt he could genuinely love someone or be worthy of anyone's love, that is, until he became a dad. His love for his kids was as profound as he was conflicted and complicated. From the songs he sang, to the music he played, to the stories he told, and the gifts he gave, every action was a demonstration of his undying commitment to his kids.

While Thomas's education, social graces, and nonconformity did not meet the standards of the average citizen, no one could ever challenge the deep, genuine love her had for his children. The love he was surrounded by in his first few years of life was evident years later in all the ways he loved his children. No matter the chaos or challenges that characterized most of Thomas's life, the love his life started with lives on today and is fondly shared with the grandchildren he never knew.

*THOMAS (SCHMIEDER) JONES was born outside Heidelberg, Germany in 1964. He died May 26, 2008, in DeRuyter, NY, after being shot several times by a New York State Trooper. The 911 call came in as a domestic violence situation involving a man with a criminal record of DWIs and a similar altercation with police officers in New Jersey several years prior. Outside of what was reported in local newspapers about the incident itself, details of the events leading up to the shooting have never been disclosed by the woman who made the 911 call. What followed in social media was as painful as the shooting itself. People with no knowledge of the man wrote opinions and passed judgment in cruel, insensitive ways while giving no thought to the five children who were left fatherless. Two of these children are his first two, my precious daughters. This story is meant to share the impact of pivotal times that contribute to both life and, sometimes, death. It is also meant to give my girls insight to the man who loved them more than any words can express.

5

SILENT RENEGADE

*a*n early morning call broke the stillness of the house. Jodi had barely wiped the sleep from her eyes. She whispered to herself, "Who could be calling at this hour?" Then she shouted, "Will someone get that phone?" No one responded, the house was empty.

Jodi did not feel like running through the house for what was likely a call for one of the girls or another irritating salesperson. When she realized the caller was determined to get an answer, she slid into her slippers and shuffled down the hall. "This had better be good!"

In a low, raspy voice she managed a curt hello. She wanted the caller to know this intrusion was quite an inconvenience. The person on the other end paused at the abruptness. Jodi's tone was stern: "Hello, who is this?"

The voice on the other end slowly explained the purpose of the call. Jodi became weak in the knees. The color drained from her face. So great was the sweat on her brow that she could feel it trickle down her temples. She took several deep breathes as she tried to process the gravity of the information, but her mind went blank.

"Jodi, this is Dr. Nathan's office. We have the results of your breast examination. We need you to come to the office today so we can begin work on our plan." The words reverberated over and over in her brain. After a minute that felt like hours, she regained her composure. She thought, "Our plan . . . what was our plan?"

Once Jodi regained her balance after that gut-wrenching blow, her thoughts raced to her family. How was she going to tell her ten-year-old twins that their mommy had cancer? Would Mark be able to carry the burden of raising the girls if this did not turn out well? The questions came like a tsunami, one crashing thought after another. After all, her sister had died just a few years earlier from the same cancer.

"Oh no, how am I going to tell mom?" She instantly snapped back to the dark day her mom came to her with the heartbreaking news that she and her dad were divorcing. For a thirteen-year-old girl, this was easily the worst day of her life. All these years later, she could still feel the sick feeling that had settled in her stomach.

That day felt like yesterday. She ran to her room, her greatest retreat. Bad Company's debut album had just come out. She threw it on the record player, turned up the volume, and belted out the lyrics to drown the ache in her heart. The songs' words seemed to tell her story. The entire album became an anthem for her life. She was not going to let her mother know the pain the news caused was a dagger to her heart.

That was a pivotal time in Jodi's life. The next few years were a steady progression of delinquency: skipping school with Catrina and her little brother, Joe, followed by stealing cars just to take joy rides on the reservation; diverting the store clerk's attention while Barbara shoplifted the newest, most popular swimsuit at the priciest downtown store; and begging for bus money from a nun to avoid hitch-hiking ten miles home.

At 5'9" Jodi towered over most of her classmates. Her hairstyle was simple, long straight hair parted down the middle, the way most girls in the 70s wore their hair. Flannel shirts, bell bottom jeans, and work boots were her typical dress, not like most girls in the 70s. Jodi was her own person with her own style.

Jodi was unusually silent and in the background. I believe this aloofness added to the "cool" factor. Others would copy whatever twist she added to her wardrobe – like the rawhide leather necklace paired with a silver chain where a St. Christopher medal hung. Jodi tested this one day by wearing a ponytail on the left and leaving the right side straight. The next day half of the eighth-grade girls came to school that way. She was amused at how gullible others were.

Jodi wasn't an angry chick; she just didn't share details about her life. She was determined to keep the walls up high enough to prevent any more hurt from crawling into her life. Rarely did she display any sort of anger or bitterness. She just moved through high school like a ghost. Everyone knew who Jodi was, but no one knew Jodi.

By ninth grade, Jodi was smoking cigarettes and weed and popping downers—nothing too serious, just enough to stay numb. Nothing hurts when you are stoned.

When you were from the south side of the city, it was best to have a rough and unapproachable reputation. The quieter you were, the more revered you became. Jodi's response to most things was a simple smile and an occasional laugh. In those rare moments where she wholeheartedly smiled, you could catch a glimpse of a little girl who was gentle and kind.

Jodi met Mark the summer after she turned fifteen. He was playing with his dogs in the park. At first, it was his long blonde hair that caught her eye, and then it was his steely blue eyes that somehow matched the color of his worn-out jeans. He seemed so carefree. Mark was several years older than Jodi. He had the same quiet disposition as she. He understood her and accepted her just as she was. They were kindred spirits.

Jodi always loved Mark but was determined not to repeat her parents' mistakes. Though they never left one another's side, they never talked of marriage or kids. After high school, life was predictable (except for marriage that is). Mark and Jodi moved in together. She worked her job at the credit union, he worked construction. Work, dogs, partying - rinse, and repeat; that was their life. This was the simplicity Jodi craved and she was happy.

In her late twenties, Jodi got the news she never dreamed possible, "Jodi, you're going to be a mom!" Oddly enough, she felt unexplainable joy. Years of emotional isolation seemed to melt right there on the spot.

Becoming a mom changed Jodi's world. From that moment on, she no longer looked for shelter in drugs and alcohol. There was no explanation for her transformation other than perhaps the notion that she now knew what love was from the inside out.

She and Mark lived a simple life, no extras but comfortable. From the moment her twin girls were born, she gave herself, all of herself, to them. Raising the girls in a simple life filled with love was paramount to issues of money, prestige, or reputation. Laughter had replaced the angry lyrics of her adolescence. Warm hugs had replaced numbing drugs. Sweet kisses had melted her thoughts of insignificance! She showed them kindness, gentleness, and peaceful ways of dealing with the world. The next ten years were the happiest of her life.

A long-standing joke as a teenager was the retched thought of one day becoming forty. How awful! The thought of getting wrinkles, turning gray, and dealing with all that sags seemed unmentionable. Funny how forty came and went without notice.

The declarations of a teenager were but whispers in the distant places of her memories.

Jodi never shared the delinquency of her youth with anyone, not even Mark. Her best friend was the only one who knew all those stories. She was the only one who knew what made Jodi tick and why. A friend so loyal that the stories would remain buried forever. What good would it do to share with Jodi's daughters her deep hurt and the loss of her childhood that drove her to such transgressions?

The stories would have been so revealing. Perhaps the girls would have understood the distance Jodi sometimes displayed. Perhaps it would have explained why she spoke so little during times of chaos or conflict. Perhaps they would have learned that it was OK to hurt when things feel bad and to share that hurt with others. These were not the lessons Jodi shared with her girls. She could never be this vulnerable, this weak.

Later that day, she tearfully broke the news to Mark. He was shaken, but quietly and calmly wrapped her in his arms. He said, "Jodi, we'll get through this like everything else we've gone through these last twenty-five years." This was the hardest moment of their entire relationship, but they knew it would be easier than telling the girls.

The next day, Jodi and Mark took the girls on a picnic to their favorite park. The dogs stayed home. The basket was filled with all their favorite foods—

peanut butter and fluff sandwiches, Cheetos, and Twinkies. Nothing healthy, just fun foods. Nothing seemed unusual about the day; the girls were used to such outings. At first, the conversation was filled with the energy ten-year-old girls bring to every situation—chattering, giggling, and sometimes a little snippiness. The family outing and the brilliant afternoon sun made for a perfect day; almost.

Jodi and Mark sat the girls down and calmly told them their mommy was sick. They did not go into the details of what the next weeks and months would be like. They explained that Mommy would not feel good on some days, but Daddy and the doctors were going to take good care of her.

Jodi intentionally did not say the "C" word—cancer. The girls were barely seven when their Aunt Jackie had passed from breast cancer, but the memories were still fresh. The last thing she wanted was for her precious babies to be consumed with the worry and fear of losing their mom. No, this was not the same as the loss that occurs with divorce, but the impact could play out the same if not approached thoughtfully.

Jodi knew with every ounce of her being that the enormous love she and Mark had for these girls would carry them through this time. She took great comfort in knowing that all would be as it should be and that she had given them the tools they needed to get to the other side of loss if that's how this turned out. Hugs, kisses, laughter, and love!

A sudden calmness came over Jodi. As a family, they would face the uncertainty ahead. The crutches of youth she used to escape pain had been replaced with a love strong enough to face the pending journey. The body may not survive, but the way she touched the souls of those little girls would.

*Jodi Beach was born in Syracuse, New York just days into 1960. She was my best friend during those impressionable junior and senior high school years. The turbulent 60s and 70s, with their radical movements addressing racial and gender inequality, the Viet Nam war, and political and social unrest, all contributed to our response to things like peer pressure, the establishment, and even issues closer to home (like divorce). After high school, we drifted apart. I was thankful we connected after our fortieth birthdays. We laughed and joked about finally making it to "old age.". Jodi passed shortly after her forty-first birthday. Sadly enough, I did not find out about her death until several years later when I tried to find her to share a fiftieth birthday wish. The sadness I experienced when I learned of her death was as if it had just happened. As I wandered through our youthful memories where we attempted to define ourselves through rebellion and nonconformity the pain of another loss was dulled.

AFTERWORD

This endeavor started after I attended a reminiscence writing class held by Robin Edgar. It was several months before my dad passed when I signed up for the class. I had no way of knowing the class would start two months after he was gone. The grief was strong. Somehow, writing about childhood memories relieved much of the sting and dulled the pain.

While putting together the outline for this book, I reserved a spot for a story titled "Summer Breeze" for my daughter-in-law, Karlene, who we tragically lost as she gave birth to my granddaughter, Madison. I wanted to pay tribute to her; however, whenever I tried to form a story that captured her essence and zest for life, I didn't get very far. Perhaps the loss is still too new or the depth of the pain from that tragedy still swallows me up. Someday, I will write that story for my son, grandchildren, and the many family members and friends who so deeply miss her and dearly loved her.

I miss every one of the five people included in *Glimpses of Tenderness*. Each had a profound impact on my life in one way or another. Birthdays, holidays, special events, and the dates of their passing remind me of the holes left in my heart when they died. The tears still come as I read these stories and relive those memories but gone is the tremendous sting from grief.

I share this handful of stories so that you may be encouraged to capture your emotional journey through grief and loss in ways that give you some comfort and peace. The hardest part is to sit with the emotions. Let yourself wander through your memories to find the essence of your loved one. Think of what made that person special and unique. Then share your stories so you, too, can show others how to convert grief into comforting memories.

ACKNOWLEDGMENTS

To Clint, my husband and best friend, who always supports me wherever my path leads.

To my children Chuck, Kaleigh, and Samantha, my grandchildren, and my Mom, who teach me each and every day so many wonderful things about life and love.

To Angie, Esther, Noell, and Rivia, my Christian sisterhood, who held me up in prayer during some of my darkest times of loss and never miss an opportunity to celebrate joyous times.

_____

I love you all to the moon and back!

_____

To Barbara Ewing who reopened my eyes to creative writing after many dormant years.

To Glenn Proctor and Cortney Donelson for reigniting my desire to complete this book, which started with a short story about my dad shortly after he passed eleven years ago. Thank you both for believing (and pushing) me!

ABOUT THE AUTHOR

Lori Myers holds a master's degree from Montreat College in Management and Leadership and a bachelor's degree in Liberal Studies from Belmont Abbey College. Outside her career in information technology, Lori writes poetry and short stories, which have appeared in the Montreat and Belmont Abbey College literary magazines and the 2020 publication, *Change, Creativity, Curiosity, and Hope in a Crisis Called Pandemic,* written by members of Writing Bootcamp Charlotte. She is also a coach who focuses on helping others discover their potential by exploring possibilities.

CPSIA information can be obtained
at www.ICGtesting.com
Printed in the USA
LVHW080231200321
681908LV00017B/390